# PIRATE MAZES

## An A-Maze-ing Colorful Adventure

# Roger Moreau

Sterling Publishing Co., Inc.
New York

## This book is dedicated to Thomas

10   9   8   7   6   5   4   3   2   1

Published by Sterling Publishing Co., Inc.
387 Park Avenue South, New York, NY 10016
© 2006 by Roger Moreau
Distributed in Canada by Sterling Publishing
c/o Canadian Manda Group, 165 Dufferin Street
Toronto, Ontario, Canada M6K 3H6
Distributed in the United Kingdom by GMC Distribution Services
Castle Place, 166 High Street, Lewes, East Sussex, England BN7 1XU
Distributed in Australia by Capricorn Link (Australia) Pty. Ltd.
P.O. Box 704, Windsor, NSW 2756, Australia

*Printed in China*

Sterling ISBN-13: 978-1-4027-3709-1
ISBN-10: 1-4027-3709-2

For information about custom editions, special sales, premium and corporate purchases, please contact
Sterling Special Sales Department at 800-805-5489 or specialsales@sterlingpub.com.

# Contents

## Suggested Use of This Book

As you work your way through the pages of this book, try not to mark them. This will enable you to experience these adventures over and over again and will also give your friends a chance to see if they have the same skills to stop the pirates and find the treasure.

**Special Warning:** When the way looks too difficult, avoid the temptation to start at the end and work your way backwards. This technique would be a violation of the rules and could result in a pirate victory.

**Cover Maze:** These pirates are laying traps to prevent you from getting the treasure that they have stolen. As soon as you land on the beach, find a clear path to the treasure and it will be yours.

# Introduction

What is a pirate? He is a sailor turned bad. He steals and plunders to get treasure. Pirates often band together, with one chosen as captain, and carry out their evil deeds aboard a fast, heavily armed ship.

The years throughout the latter part of the 1600s and the 1700s are known as the golden age of piracy. Such pirates as Henry Morgan, William Kidd, and Edward Teach (known as Blackbeard) sailed the Caribbean and along coastal waters of the new world stealing and plundering. They were not the only ones. The list is long. There were even women pirates such as Anne Bonny and Mary Read. These pirates raided towns and villages and attacked treasure-laden ships, accumulating vast amounts of treasure. Often they would bury their "booty" or treasure on some out-of-the-way island with plans to return in the future and retrieve it. A treasure map would be drawn up and it too would be hidden, with only the captain knowing of its where-abouts. Sometimes the pirates would meet an untimely fate and both treasure and map would be lost for future treasure hunters to find.

Now you're going to have a chance to find such a treasure. You'll have to step back in time, hunt for a treasure map, accumulate five important keys that are hidden along the way, set sail, and fight off a dusky crew of desperate pirates who want the same treasure that you are after. The keys are important because they will unload the treasure chest, so keep on the lookout for them in the following mazes.

This is not going to be an easy adventure, but the treasure will be worth it. You will succeed and have fun along the way.

# Pirate Dictionary

Pirates had a unique way of talking that is sometimes hard to understand, so here is a brief explanation of some of their language and terms. See if you can talk in "pirate language."

**Ahoy:** A signal to get attention. Example: "Ahoy mates, over here."

**Arrrrr:** Just a grunt or groan or a reaction to things. Sometimes a way of saying "Yes or OK." Example: "Arrrrr."

**Avast:** Stop. Example: "Avast ye scurvy dogs."

**Aye Aye:** Yes. Example: "Aye aye captain."

**Belay:** Halt or stop. Example: "Belay that ye bunch of swabs."

**Bilge Rats:** Bilge is a name for the bottom of a ship's hull. Bilge rats would be a negative description of a pirate. Example: "Get to work ye bilge rats."

**Booty:** What pirates call treasure.

**Buccaneer:** A pirate.

**Doubloons:** Spanish gold coins.

**Dusky:** Dark. A negative description of a pirate. Example: "Ye dusky dogs, get to work."

**Jolly Roger:** Pirates' name for the skull and crossbones flag.

**Landlubbers:** People who do not want to be sailors. They prefer staying on land.

**Lay To:** Hold. Don't continue. Wait for the right moment to act. Example: "Lay to mates."

**Mate:** A fellow seaman.

**Pieces of Eight:** A former Spanish peso. It corresponded to the American dollar.

**Repel Boarders:** Keep the enemy from coming aboard. Example: "Stand by to repel boarders."

**Scurvy Dogs:** A negative description of a bunch of pirates.

**Shiver Me Timbers:** Indicating such surprise that all your bones are shaking. An expression of surprise. Example: "Well, shiver me timbers, look at all that booty."

**Swab:** An awkward or clumsy pirate. Example: "Ye dirty swab, lay to."

**Swashbuckler:** Another name for a pirate. A swordsman, a bully, or boaster.

**Walk the Plank:** Forcing a sailor to walk off the end of a plank and fall into the sea. A form of final punishment to a convicted seaman.

**Ye:** You. Example: "Halt ye dusky bunch of pirates."

**Yo Ho:** A yell calling attention to yourself. A way to holler "Hurray, Hurray." Example: "Yo ho, a pirate's life for me."

# The Map Room

Hidden in this map room is a special map and key. Pirates have already searched and made a mess of everything, but have failed. You must succeed. Find a clear path to the map and key.

**Start**

# The Map

There are several islands that look like your destination—Skull Island. But which one? There is only one path to the right Skull Island. Find your way by moving through the openings that will lead you there, and then turn the map over.

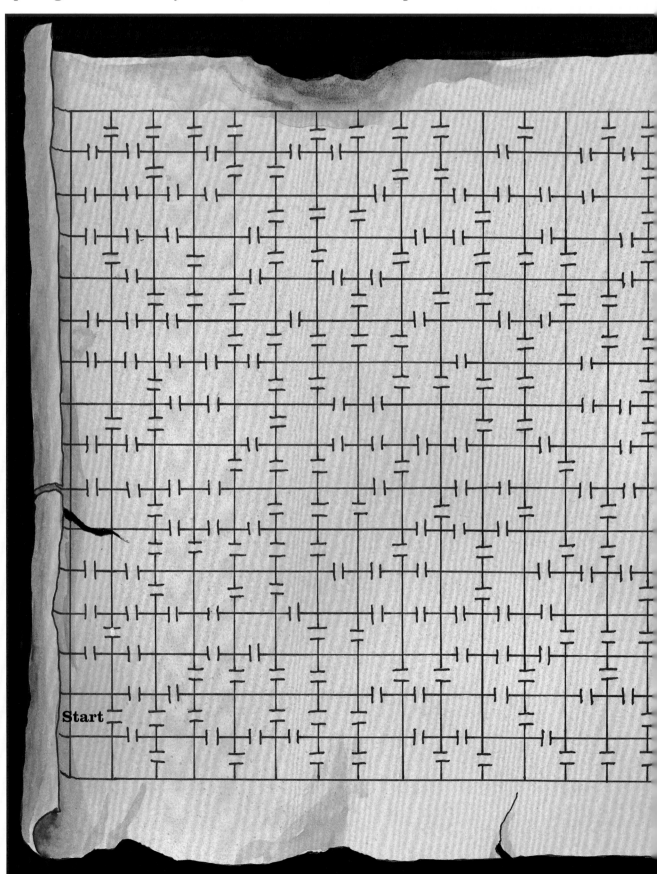

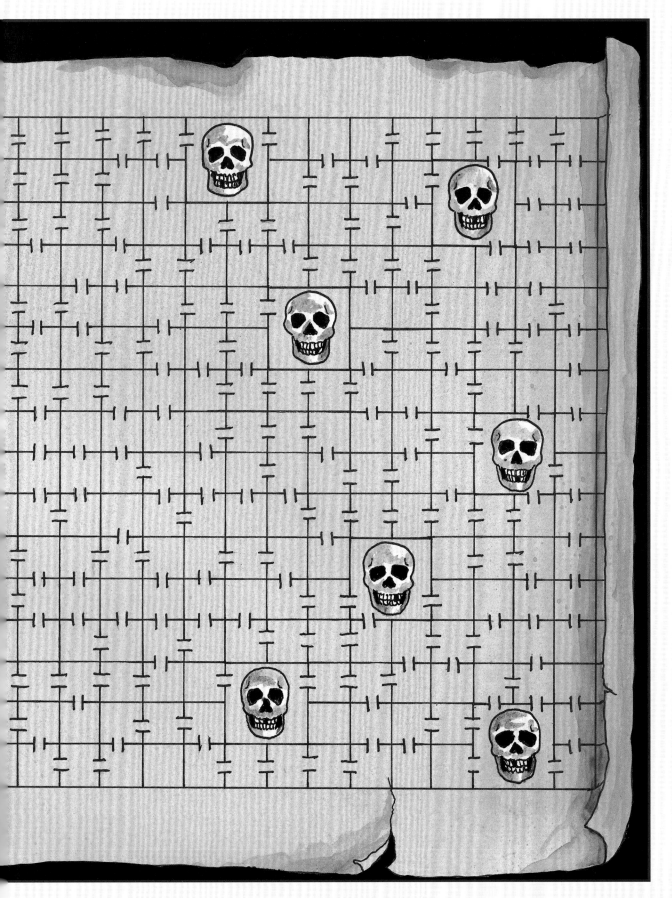

# Skull Island

On this side is a map of Skull Island. It will give you an idea of what to expect in your adventure ahead. Find a clear path, climb the ropes, and make your way to where X marks the spot.

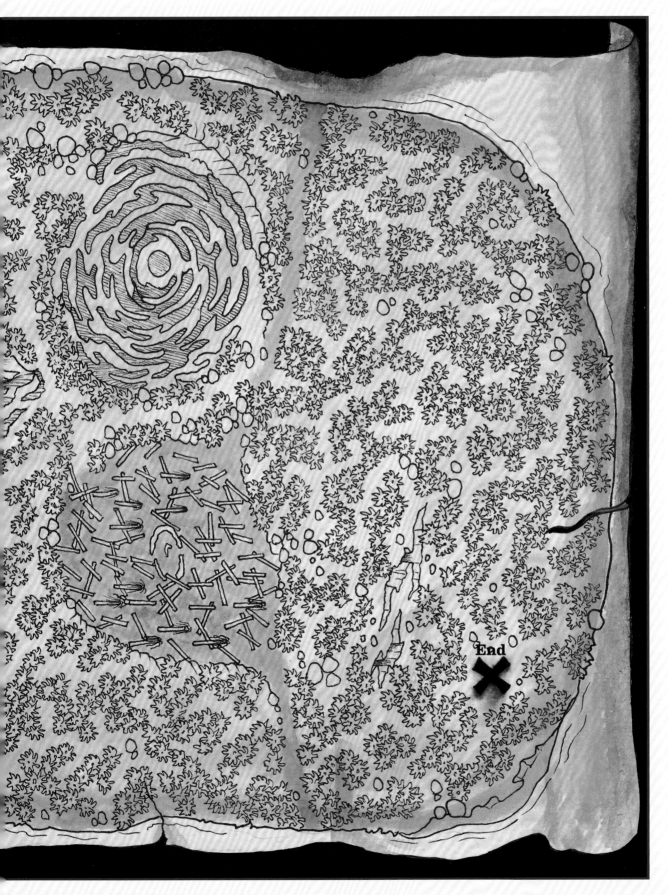

# Buccaneer Shop

Get outfitted in this shop. Find a continual path on the white tiles to each table to get your clothing, gear, and flag. Do not backtrack or move at a diagonal.

Start

End

# Buy a Ship

Buy one of these ships, but make sure it has twelve cannons, six on one side, and six on the other. Find a path between the swells.

Start

# Hire a Crew

Hire six crewmen. Be careful not to hire any pirates. In the boxes below, put a Y for "yes" (hired) and an N for "no" (not hired).

# Lower the Sails

Get ready to sail. Climb the ropes by finding a clear path.

**Start on any rope**

# Lower the Sails Continued

Continue up the ropes to the place where you can pull the rope that will lower all of the sails and you'll be underway.

# A Pirate Ship to Starboard

Off the starboard bow it looks like a pirate ship. Sail your ship to that calm spot by avoiding the waves. Then sail the pirate ship to the calm spot and be ready to do battle.

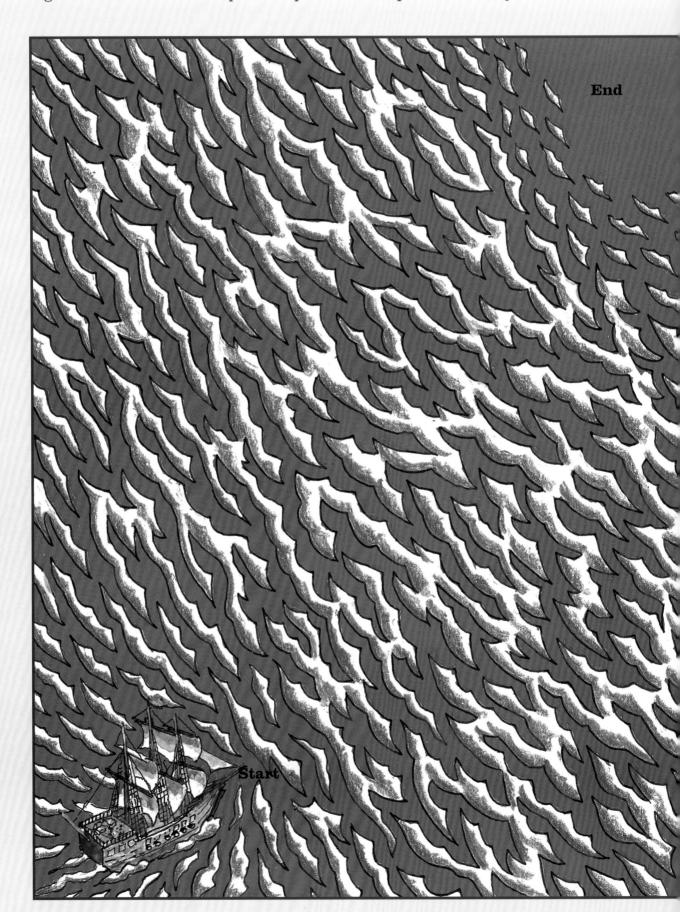

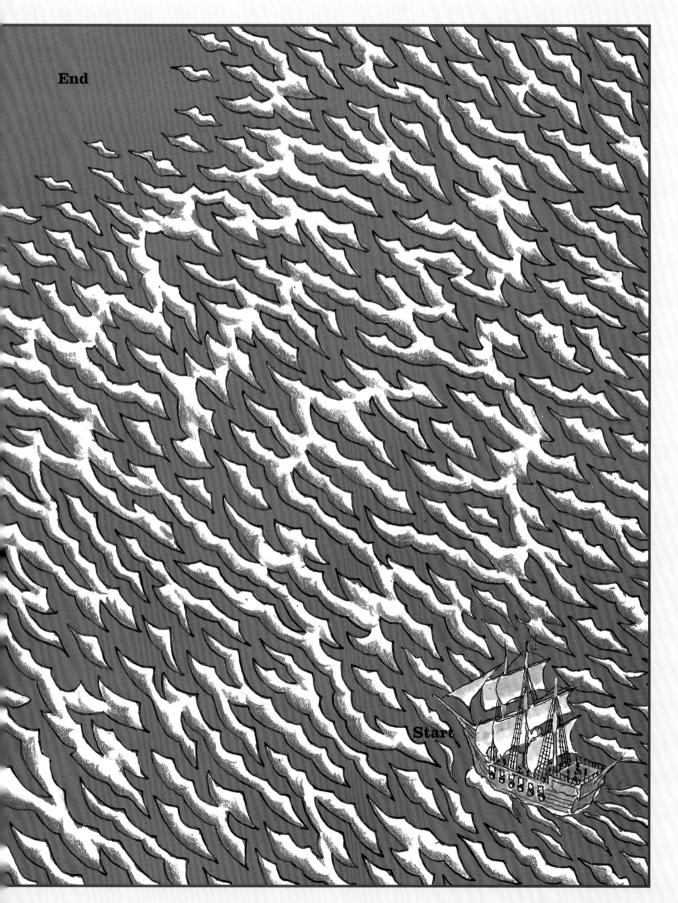

# Raise the Flag

Let the pirates know who you are by pulling on the correct rope to raise the flag. But the ropes are tangled, so identify the ropes by putting their numbers in the boxes below.

# Hoist the Skull and Crossbones

Arrrrr mates, let 'em know who we are. Raise the skull and crossbones. Place the numbers in the boxes below to pull the right rope.

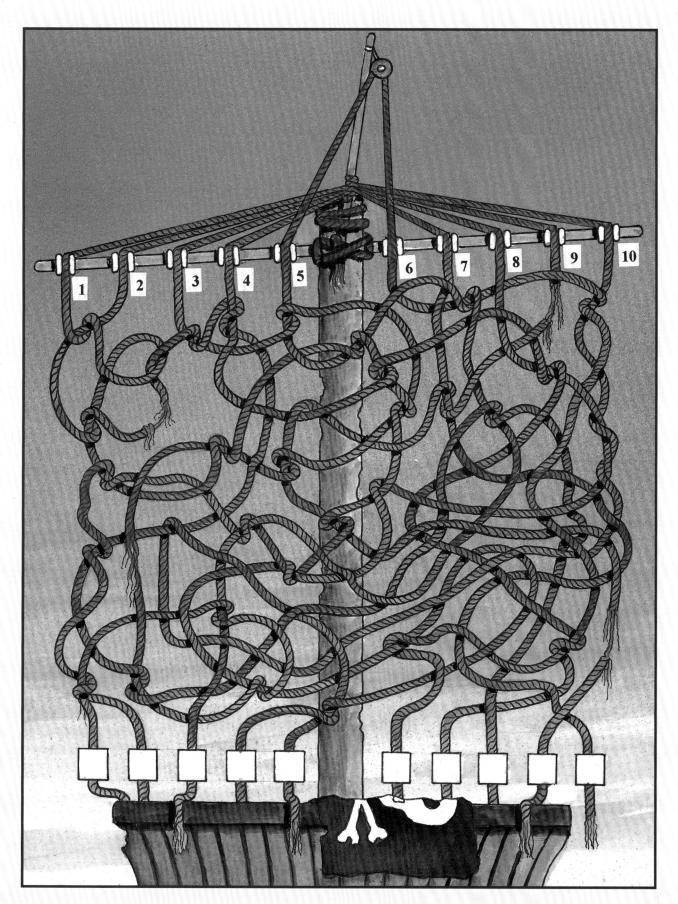

# Arm the Crew

Take the weapons to the crew by finding a clear path.

# Get Ready for Battle

"Avast ye dusky swabs and settle down. Get ready for battle." The captain will have to get them their weapons by finding a clear path to them.

# Repel Boarders

Get ready. Here they come. Stop these dusky pirates from coming on board by cutting their ropes. Find which paths will lead to the ropes and cut them.

# Get Ready to Fire

Only one cannon is left that needs cannonballs. Find a clear path and place three cannonballs by it.

Start

End

# Fire!

Four hits will sink a ship. Start at the left and take a shot by following the shot to the pirate ship. See if it's a hit or miss. Then fire a shot from the pirate ship to your ship. The first ship to get four hits sinks the opponent's ship. Good luck.

# Pick Up the Survivors

Survivors from the pirate ship are in the water. Row out to pick them up by avoiding the sharks below. Do not cross over your path and visit each survivor only once; then clap them in irons.

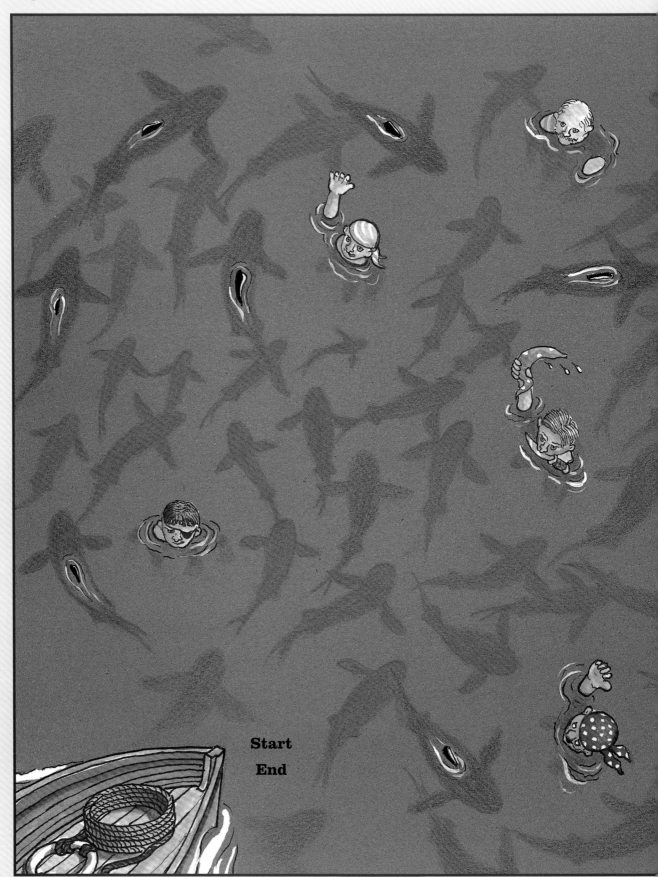

**Start**

**End**

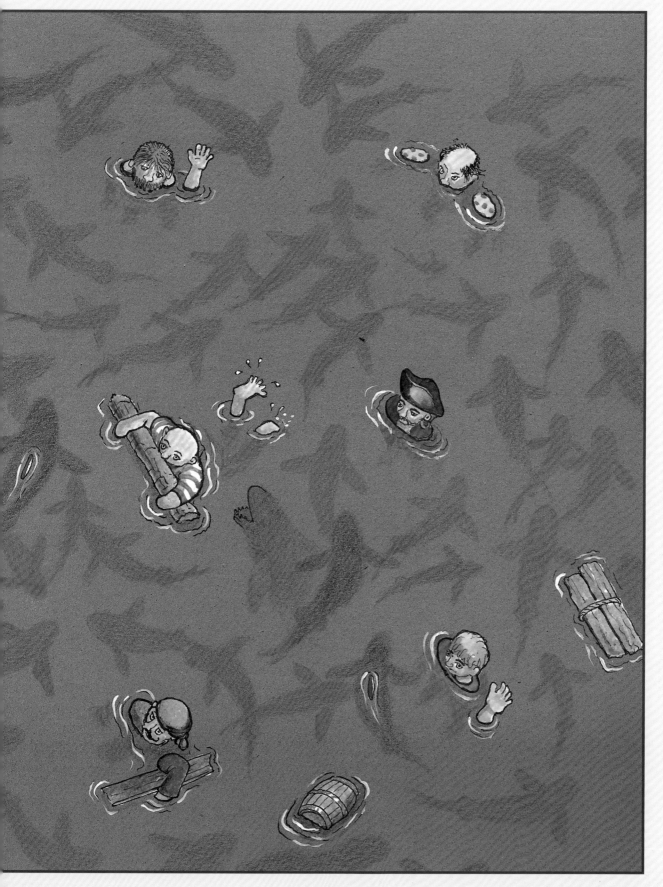

# Skull Island Ahead

Get ready to land on Skull Island by finding a clear path around the seaweed.

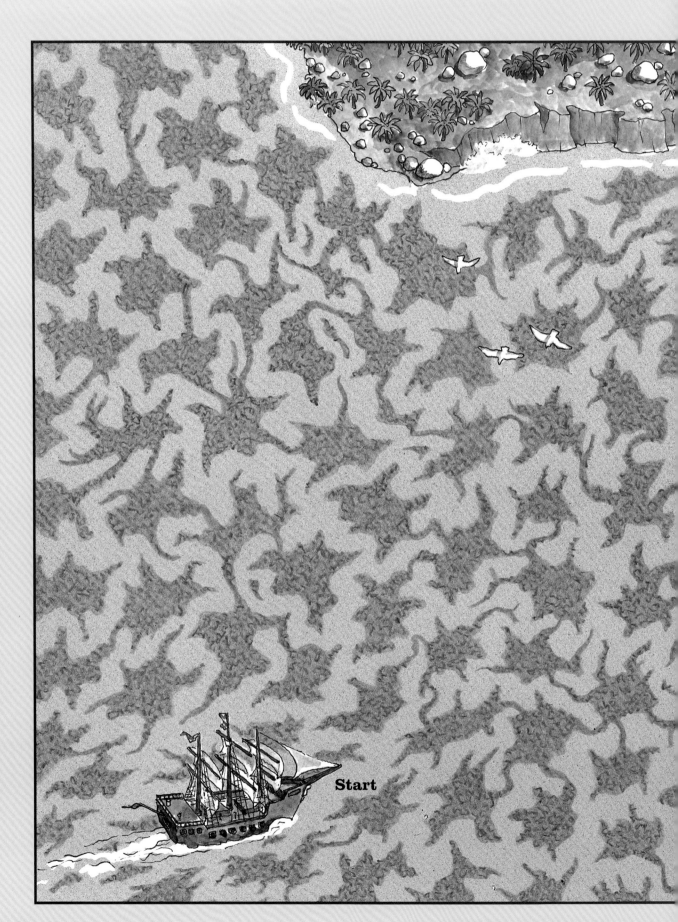

**Start**

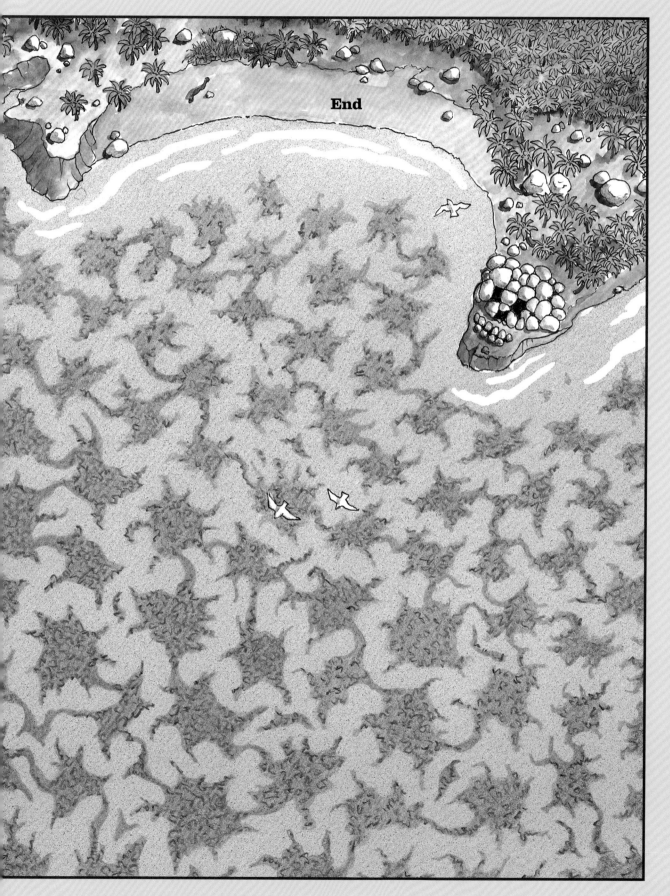

End

# Hike Inland

Find a clear path to that skeleton ahead.

Start

**End**

# Molar Mountain

Molar Mountain must be climbed. Climb the ropes to the top.

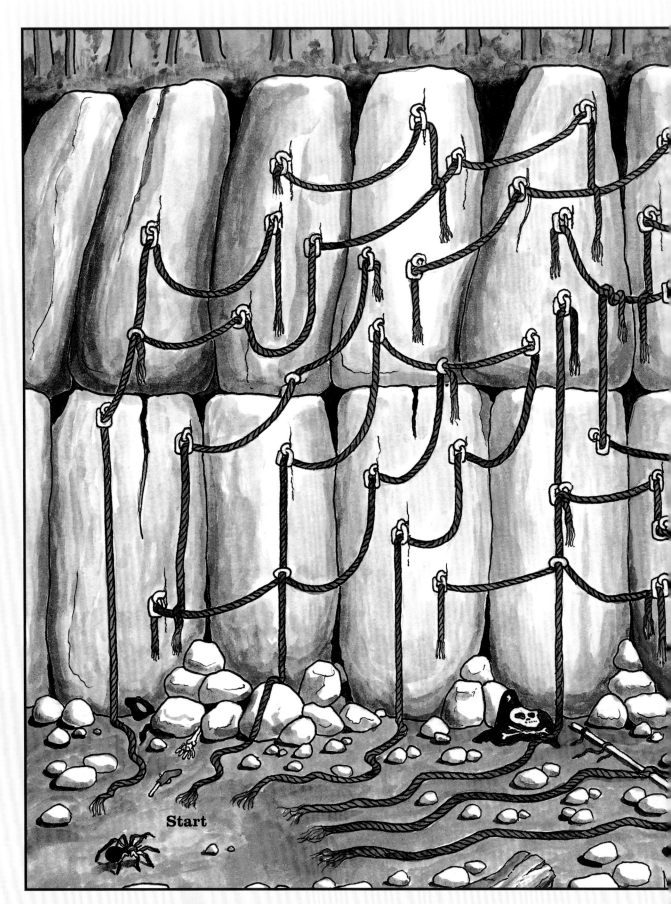

Start

**End**

# Nazal Canyon

Find your way to the other end of Nazal Canyon.

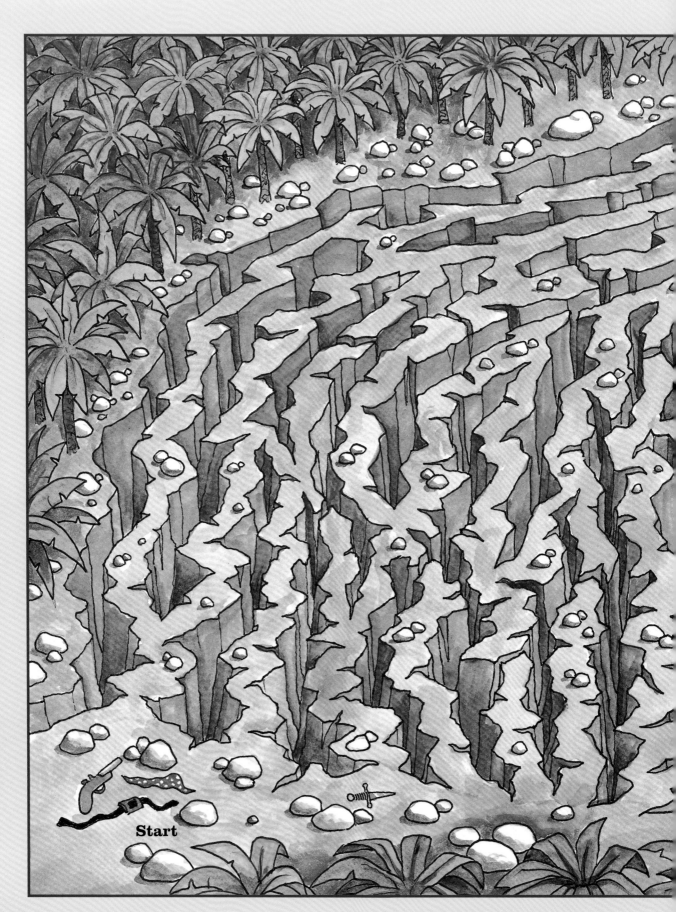

**Start**

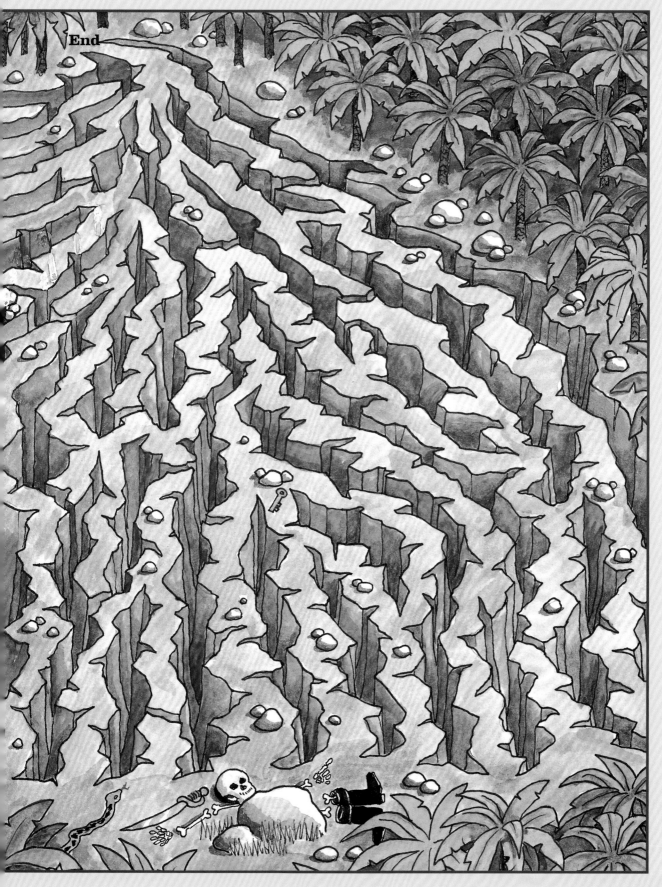

End

# Red-Eye Volcano

Red-Eye Volcano is still active. Avoid the lava and find a clear path to the other side.

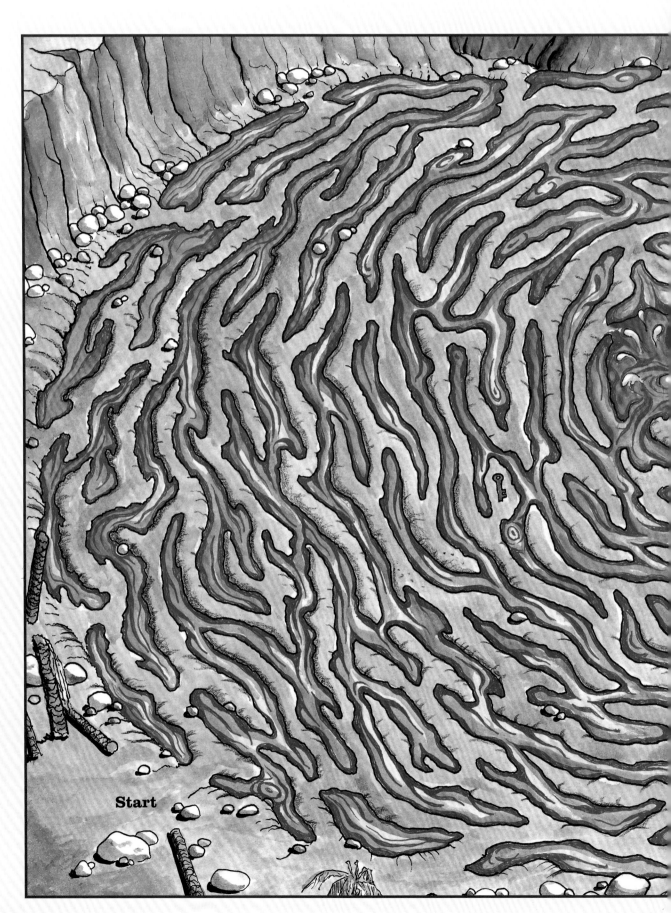

Start

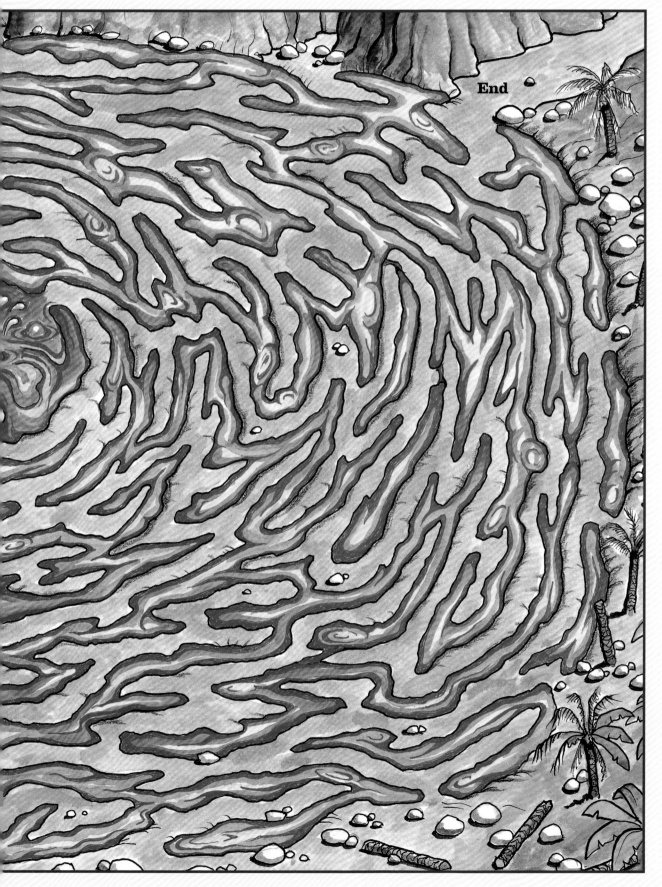

End

# Eye-Patch Volcano

This volcano has pretty much burned out. Find a clear path through it.

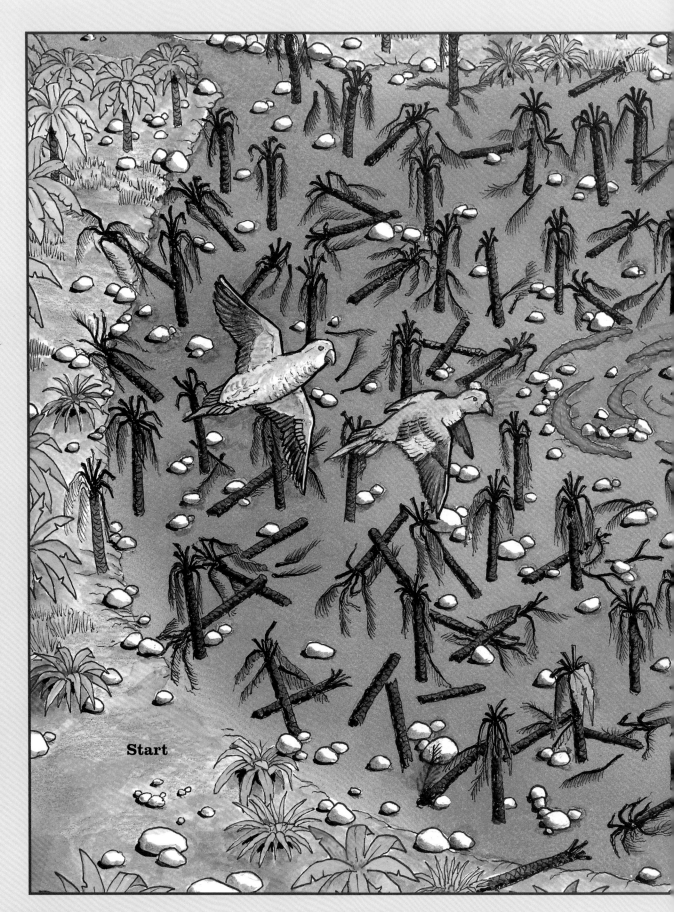

Start

End

# Oh No! More Pirates

You must be getting close to the treasure. There are pirates hiding and setting traps and trying to keep you from getting to that hole up ahead. Find a clear path and try not to be seen.

Start

End

# The Cave

Head down into this cave by finding a clear path.

Start

48

# The Cave Continued

Continue on down and use one of your keys to open the door at the bottom.

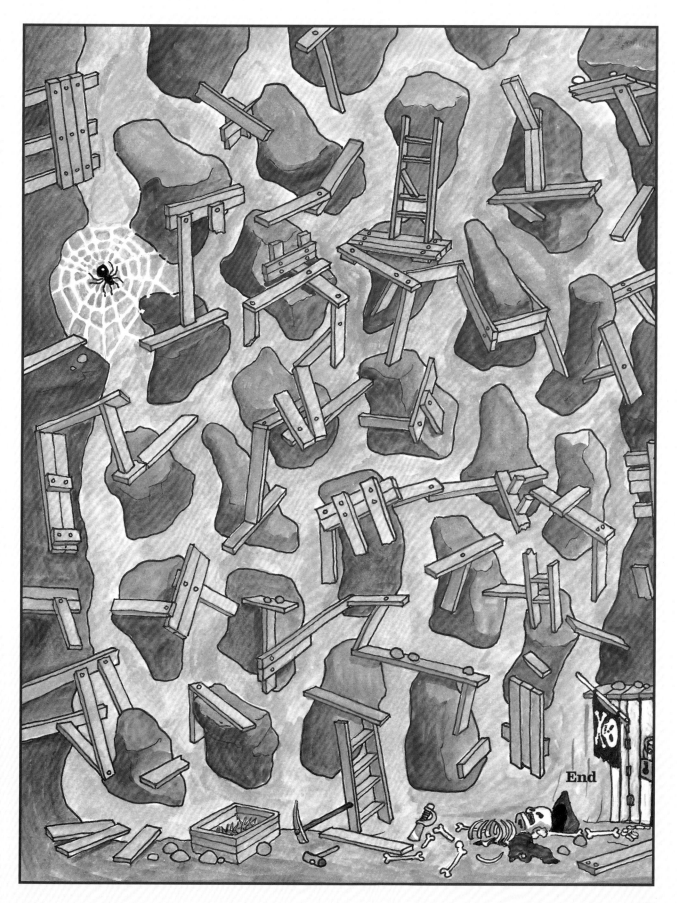

End

# The Treasure Chest

I hope you found all five keys. You've already used one and now you will need the other four to open this chest. If you haven't enough keys, you'd better go back and get what you need. Find a clear path to the chest.

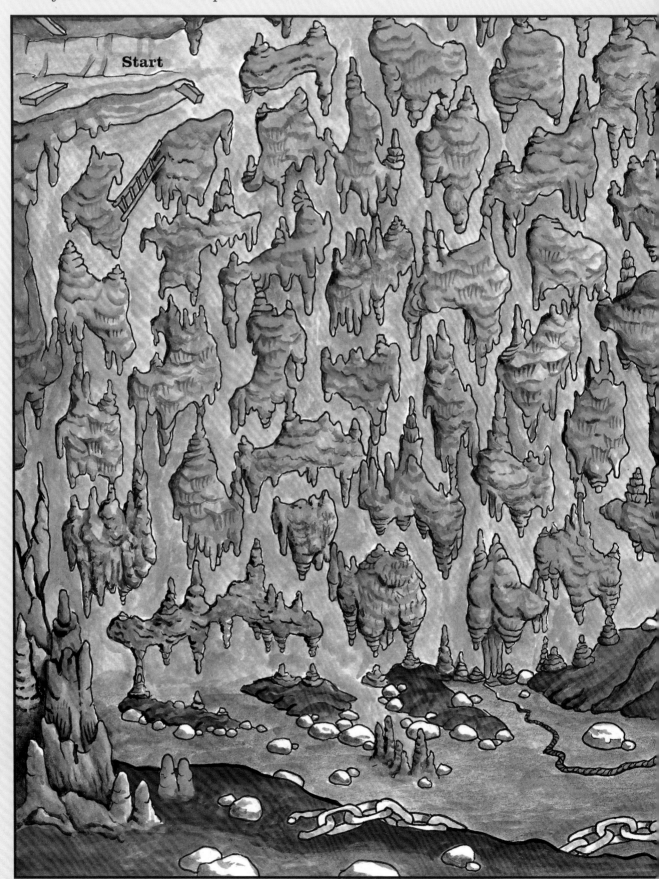

Start

End

## Congratulations

"Arrrr mate, you've done real fine. That's an awful lot of booty you've got there. I was a stowaway on your ship when ye set sail and I saw all the action. Should ye have a mind to bury that there treasure on some secret island, just give the map of its whereabouts to me and I'll safeguard it for ye. I won't tell no one either, mate. All of those scurvy dogs ye clasped in irons would make a fine crew, but I wouldn't set 'em free. No, not me. In fact, ye can trust the keys to their irons to me if ye like. You'll see, mate. Ye can trust an old has-been pirate like me, ye know. Ye sure can."

If you had any trouble along the way, the solutions to each maze are on the following pages.

**Cover Maze/The Map Room**

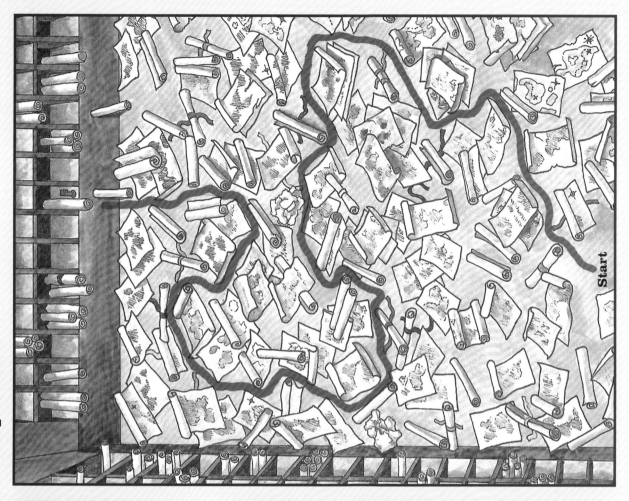

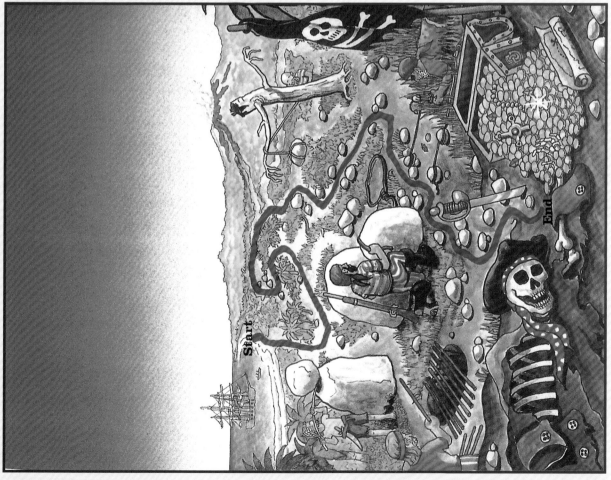

**The Map**

Start

54

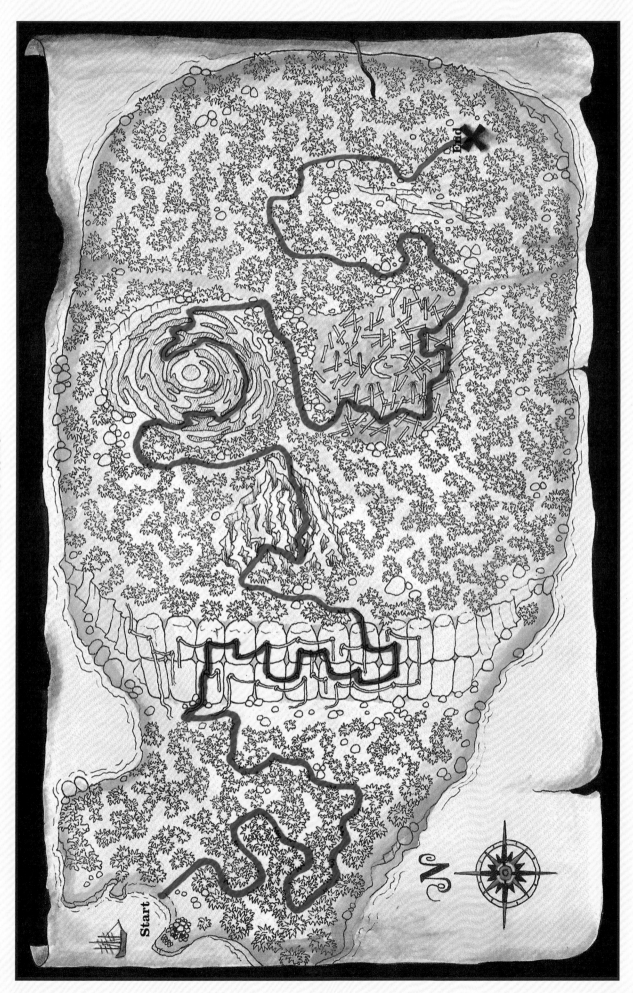

Skull Island

Start

End

55

**Buccaneer Shop**

# Buy a Ship

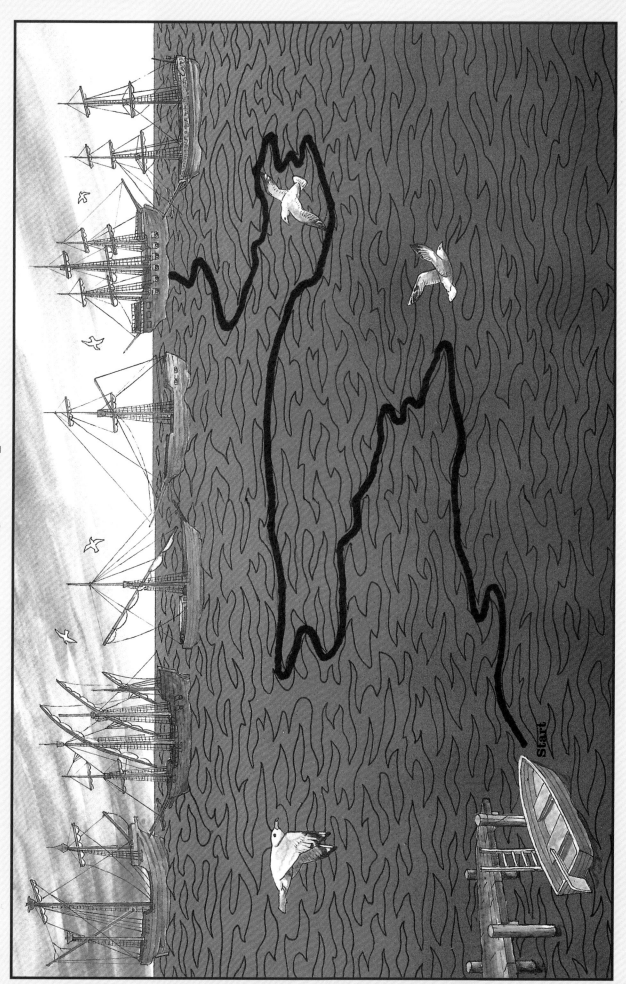

Start

# Hire a Crew

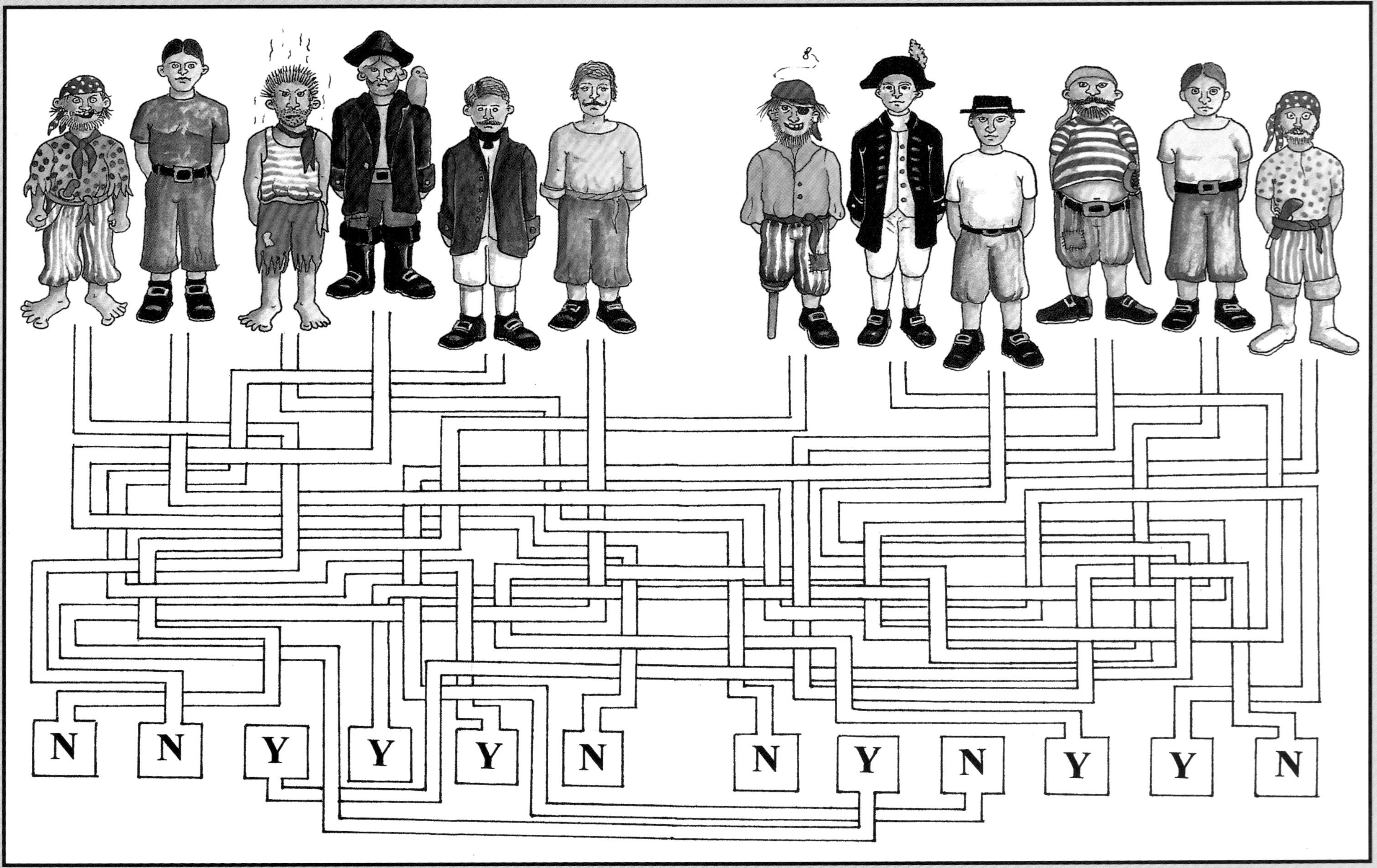

# Lower the Sails

**Start on any rope**

# Lower the Sails Continued

End

# A Pirate Ship to Starboard

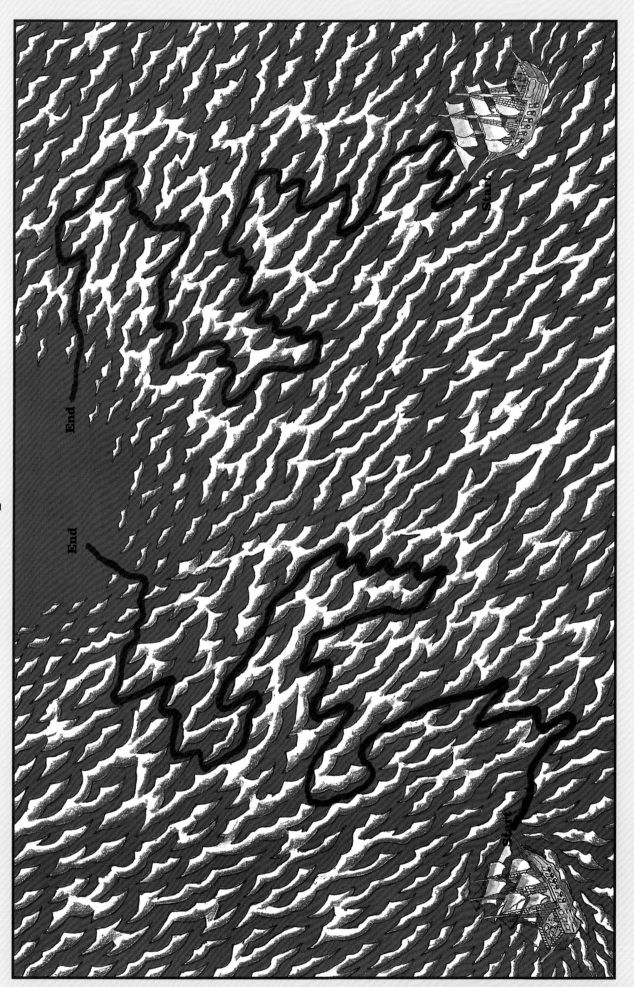

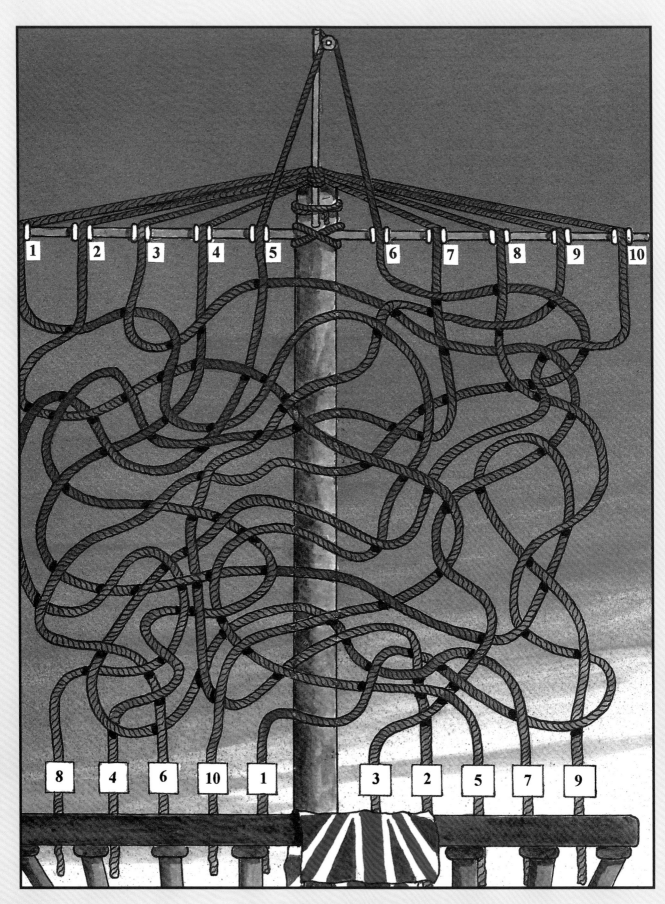

# Hoist the Skull and Crossbones

# Arm the Crew

Start

End

# Get Ready for Battle

**Repel Boarders**

# Fire!

## Pick Up the Survivors

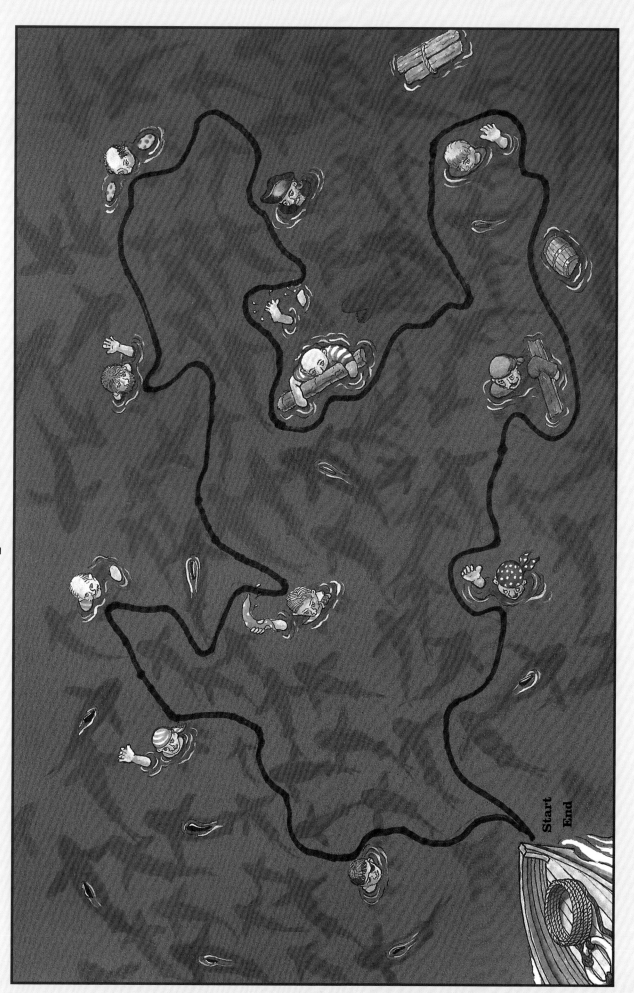

Start
End

Skull Island Ahead

End

Start

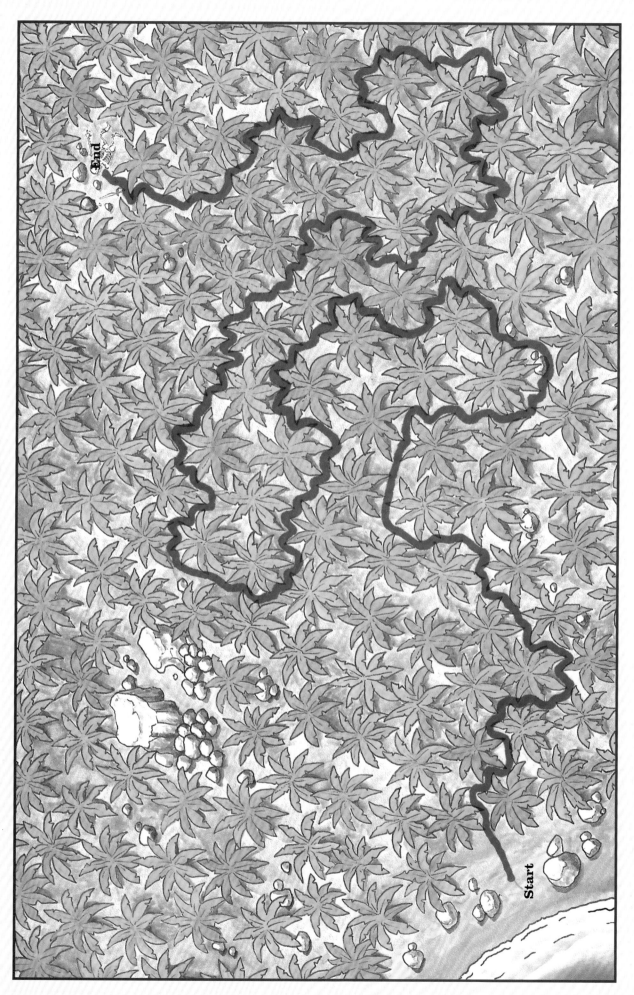

Hike Inland

# Molar Mountain

**End**

**Start**

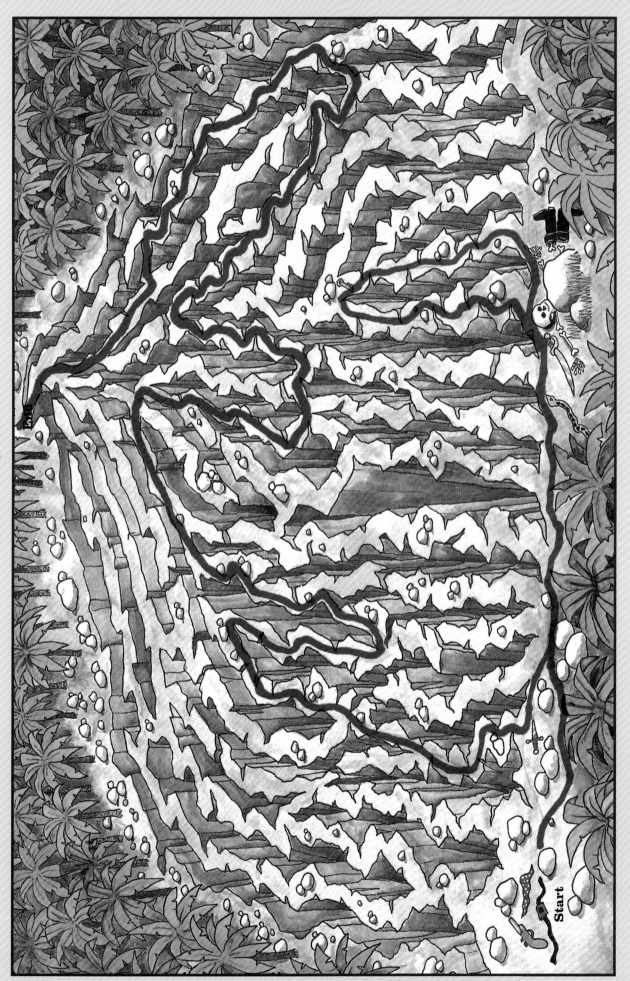

Nazal Canyon

Start

**Red-Eye Volcano**

Eye-Patch Volcano

Start

End

End

Start

# The Cave

End

# The Treasure Chest

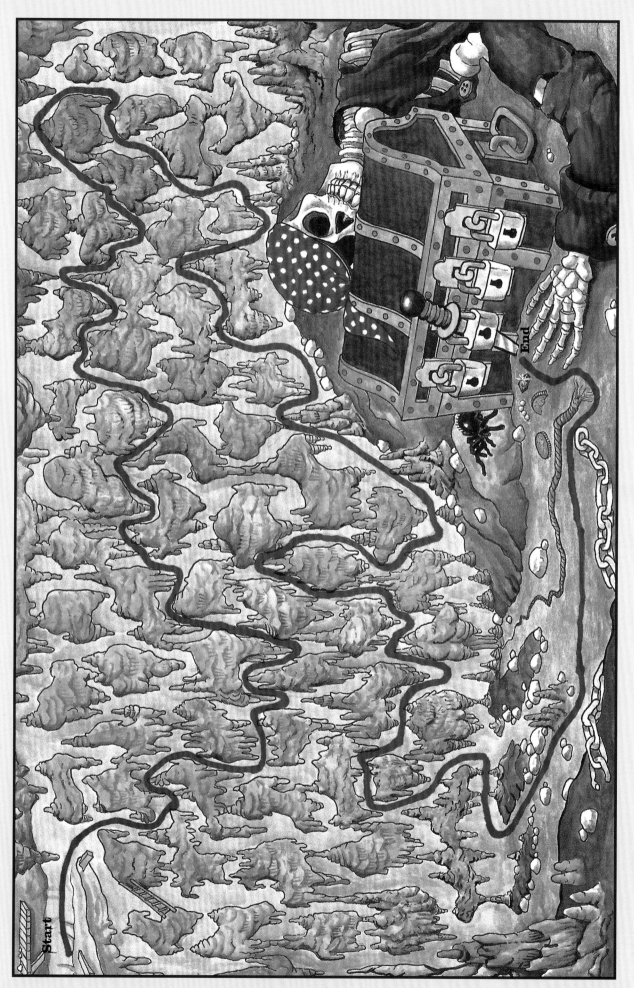

Start

End

# Index

Pages in **bold** refer to answer mazes

# Books by Roger Moreau

*Around the World Mystery Mazes: An
    A-Maze-ing Colorful Adventure!*

*Backyard Bug Mazes: An A-Maze-ing
    Colorful Adventure!*

*Dinosaur Escape Mazes: An A-maze-ing
    Colorful Adventure*

*Dinosaur Mazes*

*Great Escape Mazes*

*History Mystery Mazes: An A-maze-ing
    Colorful Adventure!*

*Lost Treasure Mazes*

*Mountain Mazes*

*Natural Disaster Mazes*

*Space Mazes*

*Treasure Hunt Mazes: An A-Maze-ing
    Colorful Journey!*

*Undersea Adventure Mazes: An A-Maze-ing
    Colorful Journey!*

*Volcano & Earthquake Mazes*

*Wildlife Mazes: An A-Maze-ing Colorful
    Journey Into the Wild!*

*Wild Weather Mazes*

*Wizard Magic Mazes: An A-Maze-ing
    Colorful Quest!*